Yellow Umbrella Books are published by Capstone Press
151 Good Counsel Drive, P.O. Box 669, Mankato, Minnesota 56002
http://www.capstone-press.com

Library of Congress Cataloging-in-Publication Data
Trumbauer, Lisa, 1963–
    Seasons/by Lisa Trumbauer; consulting editor, Gail Saunders-Smith.
    p. cm.
    Includes index.
    ISBN: 0-7368-0732-2
    1. Seasons—Juvenile literature. [1. Seasons.] I. Saunders-Smith, Gail. II. Title.
QB637.4.T74   2001
508.2—dc21   00-036477

Summary: Describes the seasons and tells what people, plants, and animals do during
each season.

Editorial Credits:
Susan Evento, Managing Editor/Product Development; Elizabeth Jaffe, Senior Editor;
    Jessica Maldonado, Designer; Kimberly Danger and Heidi Schoof, Photo Researchers

Photo Credits:
Cover: Photo Network/Michael Phillip Manheim (top left), Index Stock Imagery (top right),
Index Stock Imagery (bottom left), Unicorn Stock Photos/Tom McCarthy (bottom right); Title
Page: Index Stock Imagery; Page 2: Index Stock Imagery; Page 3: Caroline Woodham/Pictor;
Page 4: John Shaw/TOM STACK & ASSOCIATES (left), Brian Parker/TOM STACK &
ASSOCIATES (right); Page 5: Victoria Hurst/TOM STACK & ASSOCIATES (left), Kent &
Donna Dannen (right); Page 6: Daemmrich/Pictor; Page 7: Visuals Unlimited/Mark Gibson
(left), Paul Dalzell/Pictor (right); Page 8: Rob Simpson/Pictor (top left), Mike
Booher/Transparencies, Inc. (bottom left), International Stock/Mark Newman (right); Page 9:
Index Stock Imagery; Page 10: Visuals Unlimited/Mark Gibson, Photo Network/Cynthia Salter
(inset); Page 11: Photo Network/Paul Thompson, Visuals Unlimited/Bill Kamin (top inset),
Kent Knudson/Pictor (bottom inset); Page 12: David Dennis/TOM STACK & ASSOCIATES
(upper left), James P. Rowan (lower left), Pictor (right); Page 13: Shaffer Photography/James L.
Shaffer, Visuals Unlimited/Inga Spence (inset); Page 14: Index Stock Imagery, Index Stock
Imagery (inset); Page 15: John Shaw/TOM STACK & ASSOCIATES (top left), Visuals
Unlimited/Rob & Ann Simpson (bottom left), Telegraph Colour Library, FPG International
LLC (right); Page 16: Photo Network/Gay Bumgarner (all)

1 2 3 4 5 6 06 05 04 03 02 01

Seasons

by Lisa Trumbauer

Consulting Editor: Gail Saunders-Smith, Ph.D.
Consultants: Claudine Jellison and
Patricia Williams, Reading Recovery Teachers
Content Consultant: Jeff Gillman, Assistant Professor,
Department of Horticultural Sciences, University of Minnesota

Yellow Umbrella Books

an imprint of Capstone Press
Mankato, Minnesota

It's winter!
Put on a heavy coat, hat,
and gloves.
Let's go outside!

The weather is cold
and snow falls.
It's fun to play in the snow.

In winter, most trees
have lost their leaves.
Evergreen trees
keep their leaves.

On a winter day,
you may see a white rabbit.
Some rabbits grow white fur
in the winter to hide
in the snow.
Bears go into their den
to sleep through the winter.

It's spring!
Put on a light coat
and bring an umbrella.
Let's go outside!
The weather gets warm
and it rains a lot.

The spring weather
makes leaves and blossoms
grow on trees.
Spring flowers bud
and then bloom.

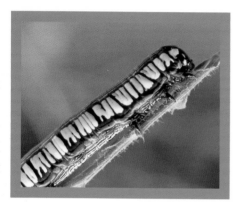

On a spring day, you may
see swans and their babies.
You may see caterpillars too.
It's warm enough for bears
to come out of their dens.

It's summer!
Put on shorts and a T-shirt,
or a swimsuit.
Let's go outside!

The weather gets hot. The sun shines brightly. It's fun to play in the sunshine!

The trees are green.

Fruits trees grow fruit.

Vegetables grow in gardens.

Summer flowers are in bloom.

On a summer day, you may
see butterflies and bees.
Baby animals grow bigger.

It's fall!

Put on a sweater and jacket.

Let's go outside!

The weather gets cool.

It's fun to pick

apples and pumpkins.

Look at the leaves on the trees.
They turn colors
and fall to the ground.
It's fun to play in the leaves.

On a fall day, you may see squirrels gather nuts for winter.
Birds begin to fly south.
Kids are back at school.

The Cycle of Seasons

winter

spring

fall

summer

After fall, it's winter again!
The cycle of seasons
goes on and on.
What's your favorite season?

Words to Know/Index

bloom—to grow flowers; pages 7, 11

blossom—a flower on a fruit tree or other plant; page 7

butterfly—an insect with a thin body and four big, colorful wings; page 12

caterpillar—the larva of a butterfly or moth; caterpillars look like worms; page 8

cycle—a complete set of events that happens again and again in the same order; page 16

evergreen tree—a tree with leaves that look like needles; evergreen trees stay green all year; page 4

swan—a large water bird with white feathers, webbed feet, and a long neck; page 8

umbrella—a frame with cloth stretched over it; umbrellas protect people from rain; page 6

vegetable—a plant grown to be used as food; people often eat vegetables as side dishes or in salads; page 11

weather—the outdoor conditions at a certain time and place; pages 3, 6, 7, 10, 13

Word Count: 282
Early-Intervention Levels: 9–12